Cupcakes for Princesses

LOVE FOOD

First published in 2009
Love Food ® is an imprint of Parragon Books Ltd

Parragon
Queen Street House
4 Queen Street
Bath BA1 1HE, UK

Copyright © Parragon Books Ltd 2009

Love Food ® and the accompanying heart device is a trademark of
Parragon Books Ltd

ISBN: 978-1-4075-6425-8
Printed in China

Designed by Emily Lewis
New photography by Sian Irvine
Home economy by Jack Sargeson
New recipes by Rachel Carter
Introduction by Cathy Jones
Edited by Theresa Bebbington

Notes for the Reader
This book uses imperial, metric, and US cup measurements. Follow
the same units of measurement throughout; do not mix imperial
and metric. All spoon measurements are level: teaspoons are
assumed to be 5 ml, and tablespoons are assumed to be 15 ml.
Unless otherwise stated, milk is assumed to be whole, eggs and
individual vegetables such as potatoes are medium, and pepper
is freshly ground black pepper.

The times given are an approximate guide only. Preparation times
differ according to the techniques used by different people and
the cooking times may also vary from those given as a result of
the type of oven used. Optional ingredients, variations or serving
suggestions have not been included in the calculations.

Recipes using raw or very lightly cooked eggs should be avoided
by infants, the elderly, pregnant women, convalescents, and
anyone with a chronic condition. Pregnant and breastfeeding
women are advised to avoid eating peanuts and peanut products.
Sufferers from nut allergies should be aware that some of the
ready-prepared ingredients used in the recipes in this book may
contain nuts. Always check the packaging before use.

The publisher would like to thank Getty Images for the permission
to reproduce images from the following pages: 1, 3, 7, 10, 24, 38
and 52.

The publisher would also like to thank Corbis for the permission to
reproduce the front cover image.

contents

let's conjure up some cupcakes!

There's a party at the palace and we need some scrumptious cupcakes and treats fit for a princess. So put on your princess apron, wash your hands, and start mixing some magic!

Baking cupcakes is such fun, and it's even more fun if you can do it with someone else. All the recipes in this book have been created for you to cook with the help of a Head Cook, an adult such as Mom, Dad, or your guardian.

A recipe is like a magic spell—it begins with a list of lovely things to put in your mixture. Check the palace kitchen cupboard to make sure you have everything in the recipe before you begin. You may need to get some special ingredients from a store that supplies special baking ingredients.

And like all good magic, you need just enough of everything for it to work. Carefully measure each ingredient in the recipe.

Following a recipe is easy for a dancing princess. It's just like the dancing teacher says, "Each step must follow on from the last."

Baking is like a wish—it needs exactly the right amount of time to work. Check how long the baking will take and set your kitchen timer or check the clock. Remember to put the oven on first, so that it has time to get hot. Ask Head Cook to put your cupcakes in the hot oven—Head Cook loves to feel useful!

While you're waiting for your cupcakes to cook, do some cleaning up. Head Cook will be pleased!

Be patient; opening the oven door too early will make your cupcakes sink. Remember to turn the oven off. Let your cupcakes cool on a wire rack.

Making your cakes look pretty with frosting and sprinkles is the best part! And after all that fun, guess what? Now you can eat them! Yummy!

HERE ARE SOME COOKING
TOOLS YOU WILL NEED
(SOME MORE ARE SHOWN
ON THE PAGE OPPOSITE)
✳
saucepan
baking sheet
sifter or strainer (for
sifting and dusting)
measuring pitcher
cooling rack
electric handheld mixer
balloon whisk

mixing bowl
(to mix your magic in)

measuring cups

oven mitts
(preferably pink!)

muffin pan

wooden spoon

spatula
(to scoop up every
last dollopy drop)

rolling pin

INCLUDED AT THE BACK OF THIS BOOK ARE
TEMPLATES FOR CREATING YOUR OWN
PRINCESS PATTERNS ON CUPCAKES. THERE ARE
ALSO IDEAS FOR NAME PLATES TO ENSURE
YOUR PARTY IS FIT FOR A QUEEN!

princess kitchen etiquette

HERE ARE THE PALACE KITCHEN RULES

NO DANCING IN THE KITCHEN
(there might be hot pots or pans to tip)

DIRTY THINGS
ALWAYS wear your princess apron
(you don't want to ruin your pretty clothes)
DON'T touch anything until you have washed your hands (eugh!)
NEVER touch the oven (that's the Head Cook's job)
BEWARE royal pets (they love being around food—
but it's not hygienic!)

SHARP THINGS
ALWAYS ask Head Cook for help
(don't point the knife toward yourself)
DON'T leave sharp knives near the table edge
(they might fall off onto your foot)
NEVER pick up a knife by its sharp blade
(blades are for cutting—handles are for handling!)
BEWARE of sharp knives hiding in soapy dish-washing bowls
(you might forget they are there)

HOT THINGS
ALWAYS wear your oven mitts if you're handling anything hot
(ovens and burners stay hot after they've been switched off)
DON'T let your hair or clothes dangle near a gas burner
(that's sooo dangerous!)
NEVER leave a spoon in a saucepan while it's cooking
(the handle will get very hot)
BEWARE of anything with wires and plugs
(electricity can be dangerous)

QUICKLY WIPE UP ANY SPILLS
(or Head Cook will get in a frenzy!)

HERE ARE SOME OF THE SKILLS THAT HEAD COOK CAN SHOW YOU

- Greasing or lining cake pans
- Cracking eggs
- Sifting
- Squeezing juice
- Rubbing in butter and flour
- Kneading dough
- Rolling out dough using a floured rolling pin
- Cutting out shapes using cookie cutters
- Mixing—put a dish towel under your mixing bowl to stop it from moving as you mix
- Whipping cream
- Whisking egg whites

WHEN YOU SEE THE FOLLOWING SYMBOL, YOU NEED TO ASK HEAD COOK FOR HELP. THIS COULD BE BECAUSE A HOT OVEN, STOVETOP, ELECTRICAL APPLIANCE, SHARP KNIFE, OR SCISSORS ARE INVOLVED IN THE RECIPE PREPARATION.

basic cupcake and buttercream recipe
(to create your own special cupcakes!)

MAKES 12 CUPCAKES

FOR THE CUPCAKES
⅔ cup soft butter
⅔ cup superfine sugar
2 eggs, lightly beaten
generous ¾ cup self-
  rising flour, sifted
½ tsp vanilla extract
1-2 tbsp milk

FOR THE BUTTERCREAM
generous ¾ cup soft
  butter
3 cups confectioners'
  sugar, sifted

1 Turn on the oven to 400°F/ 200°C. Put 12 paper cupcake liners in a 12-hole muffin pan. Place the butter and sugar in a mixing bowl and beat together with a wooden spoon or electric handheld mixer for 1-2 minutes, until the mixture is pale and creamy. Gradually add the eggs and continue beating until they are all added. Fold in the flour using a metal spoon. Stir in the vanilla extract and milk.

2 Place spoonfuls of the mixture into each paper liner. Bake in the oven for 15-20 minutes, until they are lightly golden, nicely risen, and, when you press the top lightly with your finger, they spring back right away. When they are cooked, remove them from the oven and let them cool in the pan for 5 minutes, then move them to a cooling rack.

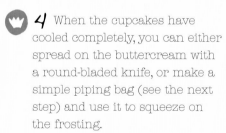

3 While the cakes are cooling make the buttercream topping. Place the butter in a bowl and, using a wooden spoon, beat together with the confectioners' sugar until you have a smooth creamy frosting.

4 When the cupcakes have cooled completely, you can either spread on the buttercream with a round-bladed knife, or make a simple piping bag (see the next step) and use it to squeeze on the frosting.

5 To squeeze on the buttercream, you can make a piping bag using a small, clean plastic food bag (the type with the ziplock top is ideal). Fill the bag with the buttercream and snip a tiny piece from one of the bottom corners with a pair of scissors. Seal the top of the bag (remove any air first), and then squeeze a swirl onto each cake.

perfect princess cupcakes!

recipes to make delicious cupcakes,
beautifully decorated, to please even
the most fussy princess.

princess cupcakes

MAKES 24 CUPCAKES

FOR THE CUPCAKES
1 cup soft margarine
scant 1¼ cups superfine sugar
4 eggs
generous 1½ cups self-rising
  white flour

FOR THE TOPPING
¾ cup butter, softened
3 cups confectioners' sugar
a variety of small candies, chocolates,
  or silver dragées (cake decoration
  balls), various colored tubes of
  decorating frosting
24 birthday cake sparklers or candles
  (optional)

sparkling decorations
will create a truly
jubilant princess

1. Turn on the oven to 350°F/180°C. Put 24 paper cupcake liners in 2 muffin pans, or put 24 double-layer paper liners on a baking sheet.

2. Put the margarine, sugar, eggs, and flour in a mixing bowl and beat together until just smooth. Spoon the batter into the paper liners.

3. Bake the cupcakes in the preheated oven for 15-20 minutes, or until golden brown and firm to the touch. Remove them from the oven and let them cool for 5 minutes in the pan, then move them to a wire rack to cool completely.

4. To make the buttercream, put the butter in a bowl and beat until fluffy. Sift in the confectioners' sugar and beat together until smooth and creamy.

5. When the cupcakes are cold, spread the buttercream on top of each cupcake, then decorate to your choice and, if desired, place a sparkler in the top of each.

pink & white cupcakes

MAKES 16 CUPCAKES

FOR THE CUPCAKES
generous ¾ cup self-rising flour
1 tsp baking powder
½ cup butter, softened
generous ½ cup superfine sugar
2 eggs, lightly beaten
1 tbsp milk
few drops red food coloring

present your cakes
with bright colors
fit for a princess

FOR THE TOPPING
1 egg white
generous ¾ cup superfine sugar
2 tbsp hot water
large pinch of cream of tartar
2 tbsp raspberry jam
3 tbsp unsweetened dried coconut,
   lightly toasted

1. Turn on the oven to 350°F/180°C. Put 16 paper cupcake liners in 2 muffin pans or put 16 double-layer paper liners on a large baking sheet.

2. Sift the flour and baking powder into a mixing bowl. Add the butter, sugar, and eggs and beat together until smooth. Mix together the milk and food coloring and mix into the mixture until evenly blended. Spoon the mixture into the paper liners.

3. Bake the cupcakes in the preheated oven for 20 minutes, or until golden brown and firm to the touch. Remove them from the oven and let them cool for 5 minutes in the pan, then move them to a wire rack to cool completely.

4. To make the topping, put the egg white, sugar, water, and cream of tartar in a heatproof bowl set over a saucepan of simmering water. Beat with a wooden spoon for 5-6 minutes, until the mixture is thick and makes soft peaks when the wooden spoon is lifted out.

5. Spread a layer of raspberry jam over each cupcake, then swirl over the topping. Sprinkle with the toasted coconut.

warm strawberry cupcakes (baked in a teacup)

MAKES 6 CUPCAKES

FOR THE CUPCAKES
8 tbsp butter, softened, plus
   extra for greasing
4 tbsp strawberry conserve
generous ½ cup superfine sugar
2 eggs, lightly beaten
1 tsp vanilla extract
generous ¾ cup self-rising
   white flour

TO DECORATE
1 lb/450 g small, whole fresh
   strawberries
confectioners' sugar, sifted,
   for dusting

sprinkle fairy dust
with your wand for
that extra magic
princess sparkle

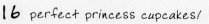

1. Turn on the oven to 350°F/180°C. Grease 6 heavy teacups with butter. Spoon 2 teaspoons of the strawberry conserve into the bottom of each teacup.

2. Put the butter and sugar in a mixing bowl and beat together until light and fluffy. Gradually add the eggs, beating well after each addition, then add the vanilla extract. Sift in the flour and, using a large metal spoon, fold it into the mixture. Spoon the batter into the teacups.

3. Stand the cups in a roasting pan, then pour in enough hot water to come one third of the way up the sides of the cups. Bake in the preheated oven for 40 minutes, or until golden brown and firm to the touch. Remove them from the oven and let them cool for 2-3 minutes in the pan, then move them to a wire rack to cool completely.

4. Place a few strawberries on each cake, then dust with confectioners' sugar and serve warm with more strawberries.

sweetheart cupcakes

MAKES 16 CUPCAKES

FOR THE CUPCAKES
scant ½ cup soft butter
½ cup superfine sugar
2 eggs, lightly beaten
scant 1 cup self-rising flour, sifted
½ tsp vanilla extract
1-2 tbsp milk

TO DECORATE
confectioners' sugar, for dusting
9 oz/250 g rolled white fondant
3 tbsp honey, warmed
red food coloring

perfect hearts for
a perfect princess

1. Turn on the oven to 400°F/200°C. Put 16 paper cupcake liners in 2 muffin pans or put 16 double-layer paper liners on a large baking sheet.

2. Put the butter and superfine sugar into a mixing bowl and beat together for 1-2 minutes, until pale and creamy. Gradually add the eggs and continue beating. Fold in the flour, using a metal spoon. Stir in the vanilla extract and milk.

3. Put a spoonful of the mixture into each paper liner. Bake in the preheated oven for 15-20 minutes, or until golden brown and firm to the touch. Remove them from the oven and let them cool for 5 minutes in the pan, then move them to a wire rack to cool completely.

4. To decorate, dust the counter with some confectioners' sugar. Roll out just over two thirds of the fondant to 8 x 11 inches/20 x 28 cm. Use a 2½-inch/6-cm round cutter to stamp out 16 circles. Using a pastry brush, lightly brush the tops of the cooled cakes with a little honey. Stick the fondant circles on top of each one.

5. To make the hearts, add a few drops of the food coloring to the remaining fondant and knead until an even red color. Roll out the fondant and cut out 16 small hearts using the heart template at the back of this book. Stick the hearts onto the cakes, using a little blob of honey to make them stay.

big cupcake princess cake

MAKES ABOUT 24 REGULAR CUPCAKES
 AND 12-18 MINI CUPCAKES

FOR THE CUPCAKES
generous ¾ cup soft butter
1 cup superfine sugar
4 eggs, lightly beaten
1¾ cups self-rising flour, sifted
½ tsp vanilla extract
1-2 tbsp milk

TO DECORATE
confectioners' sugar,
  for the frosting and dusting
rolled white fondant
pink food coloring
pink sugar balls, pink sugar crystals,
  pink and white cake decorating
  flowers, pink and white candies, and
  pink and silver edible glitter
2-3 tbsp honey, warmed

TO TOP THE CAKE
toy tiara and wand
pink streamers
mini sparklers

tiered cupcakes
for a special
tiara-wearing
princess

1. Turn on the oven to 400°F/200°C. Line two 12-cup muffin pans with regular paper cupcake liners and two 12-cup mini muffin pans with mini paper cupcake liners.

2. Put the butter and superfine sugar into a mixing bowl and beat together with a wooden spoon for 1-2 minutes, until the mixture is pale and creamy. Gradually add the eggs and continue beating until all the eggs are added. Fold in the flour using a metal spoon. Stir in the vanilla extract and milk.

3. Put a spoonful of the mixture into each paper liner. Bake both the regular size and mini cupcakes in the preheated oven for 12-15 minutes, until golden brown and firm to the touch.

4. Remove them from the oven and let them cool for 5 minutes in the pan, then move them to a wire rack to cool completely.

5. Decorate the regular size cupcakes first by rolling out some of the fondant (use a little confectioners' sugar to dust the counter first). Use the heart template at the back of this book to cut out hearts, then use the hearts to decorate about one fourth of the regular size cakes.

CONTINUED ON NEXT PAGE   perfect princess cupcakes!

Sprinkle them with the edible glitter. Use the heart template to dust heart shapes onto another one fourth of the cakes, using sifted confectioners' sugar.

6. Add some pink food coloring to the remaining fondant and knead it in well to get an even color. Roll it out thinly and cut out hearts with the heart template. Stick these onto the remaining regular cupcakes, using a dab of warm honey. Decorate with the edible glitter.

7. Next make the frosting. Sift some confectioners' sugar into a bowl and combine with a couple of teaspoons of water until you have a thick paste. (Make plenty so that you have some left over to color pink to finish decorating the mini cakes.) Use a teaspoon to spread it over about half the mini cakes, then decorate each with a pink candy and some pink glitter.

8. Finally, decorate the remaining mini cakes by adding some pink coloring to the leftover frosting. Spread it over the rest of the mini cakes and decorate each with white candies, silver balls, and/or edible silver glitter.

9. Put the cakes on the stand, putting the white decorated cakes on one side and the pink ones on the other. Pile the mini cakes on the top and stack on top of the other cakes. Top with the tiara, wand, streamers, and sparklers.

TO MAKE THE CAKE STAND
3 round cake boards in different sizes covered in pretty pink wrapping paper, edged with ribbon
2 cake "dummies" covered in ribbon (to hold up the cake boards)

party princess!

from cute cucumber sandwiches to
magnificent milkshakes, recipes for a
delicious princess party.

mini cucumber sandwich triangles

MAKES ENOUGH TO SERVE 8-10
20 thin slices whole wheat bread
soft butter
½ cucumber

👑 1. Cut off the crusts from the bread and discard (or let Head Cook have them to make into breadcrumbs). Lightly butter each slice of bread.

👑 2. Remove the skin from the cucumber (using a potato peeler is the safest way to do this), then cut into very thin slices.

👑 3. Place some slices of cucumber onto a slice of bread, top with another slice of bread, and then cut into 4 squares. Cut each square into 2 triangles, repeat with the remaining bread, and make the rest of the sandwiches in the same way.

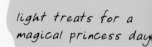

light treats for a magical princess day

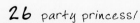

mini chocolate pinwheel sandwiches

MAKES ENOUGH TO SERVE 8-10
10 thin slices bread (white or
 whole wheat)
soft butter
chocolate spread

1. Roll each bread slice lightly with a rolling pin.

2. Spread each slice lightly with a little butter and some chocolate spread. Cut off the crusts.

3. Roll up each slice tightly into a roll, then cut into small pinwheels.

strawberry heart sandwiches

MAKES ENOUGH TO SERVE 8-10
20 thin slices white bread
soft butter
strawberry jam

1. Spread the bread slices with a little butter and spread with the jam. Sandwich together with another slice of bread and press down well.

2. Use the heart template at the back of this book (or a heart-shaped cookie cutter) to cut out hearts from each sandwich.

princess shortbread wands

MAKES 12 WANDS

FOR THE SHORTBREAD
1½ cups all-purpose flour
scant ½ cup superfine sugar
scant ½ cup cold butter
1 tbsp milk

TO DECORATE
1 egg white, lightly beaten
pink pearl sugar balls
pink edible glitter/luster
pink sprinkles

FOR THE WANDS
12 ice-cream sticks or
   wooden skewers

sweet wands to
bring magic to a
sweet princess

👑 1. Turn on the oven to 325°F/160°C. Line 2 baking trays with parchment paper.

👑 2. Put the flour and sugar into a mixing bowl and mix well with a round-bladed knife. Add the butter and use the knife to cut it into small pieces. Use your fingertips to rub the butter into the flour until it looks like breadcrumbs.

👑 3. Stir in the milk. Use the knife to mix it together, then use your hands to form the dough into a ball. Knead gently, then place on a lightly floured counter. Roll the dough to ¼ inch/ 5 mm thick, then use the heart template at the back of this book to cut out 12 hearts.

👑 4. Put the hearts on the baking trays. Press a small wooden ice-cream stick or skewer into each one (with the pointy end in the dough) and cover the wooden 'handles' with aluminum foil so that they don't burn during cooking. Bake in the preheated oven for 15-20 minutes, or until golden brown and firm to the touch. Remove from the oven and move to a wire rack to cool.

5. To decorate, brush the cookies with the egg white and sprinkle the decorations of your choice over them. Let cool.

chocolate marshmallow slices

MAKES 18 SLICES

12 oz/350 g graham crackers
4½ oz/125 g semisweet chocolate,
  broken into pieces
1 cup butter
2 tbsp superfine sugar
2 tbsp unsweetened cocoa powder
2 tbsp honey
⅔ cup mini marshmallows
½ cup white chocolate chips

what can be more
delightful, for a
princess so likeable

1. Put the graham crackers in a plastic bag, seal the bag, and, using a rolling pin, crush the crackers into small pieces.

2. Put the chocolate, butter, sugar, cocoa, and honey in a pan and gently heat until melted. Remove from the heat and let cool slightly.

3. Stir the crushed crackers into the chocolate mixture until well mixed. Add the marshmallows and mix well, then finally stir in the chocolate chips.

4. Turn the mixture into an 8-inch/20-cm square cake pan and lightly smooth the top. Put in the refrigerator and let chill for 2-3 hours, until set. Cut into slices before serving.

princess donuts

MAKES 10 DONUTS

10 ring or small jam-filled,
  plain donuts

FOR THE TOPPING
2-3 tsp water
1¾ cups confectioners' sugar, sifted
2-3 drops pink food coloring (or 1-2
  drops red food coloring)
chocolate sprinkles, pink/silver edible
  glitter, and/or pink sprinkles

small bites
of pleasure, a
princess will
surely treasure

1. Make the frosting by gradually adding the water to the
confectioners' sugar until you create a smooth but
thick consistency.

2. Use the bowl of a teaspoon to spread the frosting over the
tops of the donuts to make a good, smooth coating.

3. Sprinkle your chosen decorations over them and let the
frosting set for about 30 minutes.

ice-cream cookie sandwiches

MAKES ABOUT 30 COOKIE SANDWICHES

FOR THE COOKIES
1 cup butter, softened
scant 3/4 cup golden superfine sugar
1 egg yolk, lightly beaten
2 tbsp finely chopped preserved ginger,
 plus 2 tsp syrup from the jar
2 1/4 cups all-purpose flour
1/4 cup unsweetened cocoa powder
1/2 tsp ground cinnamon
pinch of salt

FOR THE FILLING
2 cups vanilla, chocolate,
 or coffee ice cream

a little bit of spice
for a true princess
is always nice

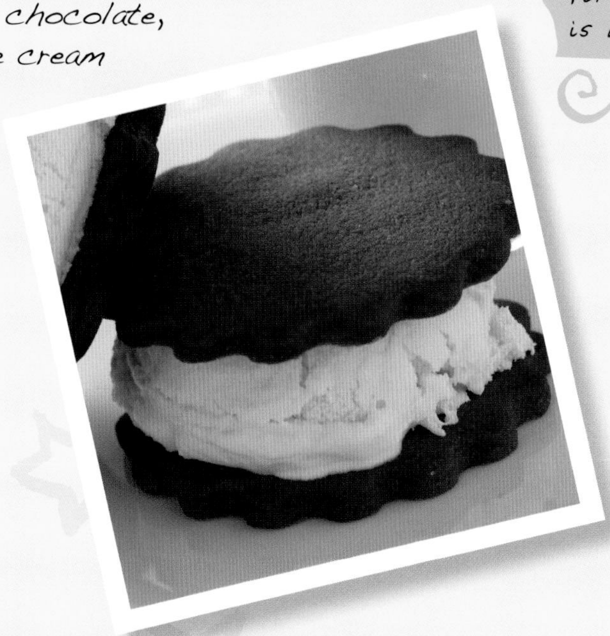

1. Put the butter and sugar into a mixing bowl and mix together, then beat in the egg yolk, ginger, and ginger syrup. Sift together the flour, cocoa, cinnamon, and salt into the mixture and stir until thoroughly combined. Halve the dough, shape into balls, wrap in plastic wrap, and chill in the refrigerator for 30-60 minutes.

2. Turn on the oven to 375°F/190°C. Line 2 cookie sheets with parchment paper.

3. Unwrap the dough and roll it out between 2 sheets of parchment paper. Stamp out cookies with a 2½-inch/6-cm fluted cutter and put them on the cookie sheets, spaced apart. Bake for 10-15 minutes, until golden. Remove them from the oven and let them cool for 10 minutes in the pan, then move them to a wire rack to cool completely.

4. Remove the ice cream from the freezer 15 minutes before serving to let it soften. Put a scoop of ice cream on half of the cookies and top with the remaining cookies.

strawberries & cream milkshake

SERVES 2

FOR THE MILKSHAKES
1 cup frozen strawberries
scant ½ cup light cream
generous ¾ cup cold whole milk
1 tbsp superfine sugar

TO DECORATE
mint leaves

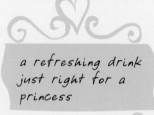

a refreshing drink just right for a princess

1. Put the strawberries, cream, milk, and sugar into a food processor or blender and process until smooth.

2. Pour into glasses and serve decorated with mint leaves.

pretty princess cupcakes!

lemon, vanilla, and cherry cupcakes, beautifully decorated with rosebuds, butterflies, and candies.

rosebud cupcakes

MAKES 12 CUPCAKES

FOR THE CUPCAKES
scant ½ cup soft butter
½ cup superfine sugar
2 eggs, lightly beaten
scant 1 cup self-rising flour, sifted
½ tsp vanilla extract
1-2 tbsp milk

TO DECORATE
confectioners' sugar, for dusting
8 oz/225 g rolled white fondant
3 tbsp honey, warmed
2-3 drops pink food coloring
tube of green writing frosting

a sweet rose that will make a perfect princess gift

1. Turn on the oven to 400°F/ 200°C. Put 12 paper liners into a 12-cup muffin pan. Put the butter and superfine sugar into a mixing bowl and beat together for 1-2 minutes, until pale and creamy. Gradually add the eggs and continue beating. Fold in the flour using a metal spoon. Stir in the vanilla extract and milk.

2. Put a spoonful of the mixture into each liner. Bake in the preheated oven for 15-20 minutes, or until golden brown and firm to the touch. Remove them from the oven and let them cool for 5 minutes in the pan, then move them to a wire rack to cool completely.

3. Dust the counter with some confectioners' sugar. Roll out all but one eighth of the fondant to 11 x 8 inches/28 x 20 cm. Use a cookie cutter to stamp out 12 circles. Brush the cake tops with some honey and stick on the circles.

4. For the rosebuds, knead the remaining fondant with the food coloring. Roll out strips of fondant to 2½ x ½ inch/6 x 1 cm. Roll up from one end and stick onto the cake with a dab of honey. Draw on a stalk and leaves with the writing icing.

lemon meringue cupcakes

MAKES 4 CUPCAKES

FOR THE CUPCAKES
6 tbsp butter, softened, plus
  extra for greasing
scant ½ cup superfine sugar
finely grated rind and juice of
  ½ lemon
1 large egg, lightly beaten
scant ⅔ cup self-rising flour
2 tbsp lemon curd

FOR THE MERINGUE
2 egg whites
generous ½ cup superfine sugar

a tangy treat for
a princess feast

1. Turn on the oven to 375°F/190°C. Grease four 1-cup ovenproof bowls (such as ramekins) with butter.

2. Put the butter, sugar, and lemon rind into a mixing bowl and beat together until light and fluffy. Gradually beat in the egg. Sift in the flour and, using a metal spoon, fold into the mixture with the lemon juice. Spoon the mixture into the bowls.

3. Put the bowls on a baking sheet and bake in the preheated oven for 15 minutes, or until golden brown and firm to the touch.

4. While the cupcakes are baking, make the meringue. Put the egg whites in a clean grease-free bowl and, using a handheld electric mixer, mix until stiff. Gradually whisk in the superfine sugar to form a stiff and glossy meringue.

5. When the cupcakes are cooked, remove from the oven and spread the lemon curd over the hot cupcakes, then swirl over the meringue. Return the cupcakes to the oven for 4-5 minutes, until the meringue is golden. Serve immediately.

mini cherry & choc sundae cupcakes

MAKES 36 MINI CUPCAKES

FOR THE CUPCAKES
scant ½ cup soft butter
½ cup superfine sugar
2 eggs, lightly beaten
scant 1 cup self-rising flour
1 tsp vanilla extract

TO DECORATE
¾ cup soft butter
3 cups confectioners' sugar, sifted
1¾ oz/50 g milk chocolate, melted
18 candied cherries, halved

sweet cherries for
a sweet princess

👑 1. Turn on the oven to 400°F/ 200°C. Put 12 mini paper liners into three 12-cup mini muffin pans.

2. Put the butter and superfine sugar into a mixing bowl and beat together for 1-2 minutes, until pale and creamy. Gradually add the eggs and continue beating. Fold in the flour using a metal spoon. Stir in the vanilla extract.

👑 3. Put a teaspoonful of the mixture into each paper liner. Bake in the preheated oven for 12-15 minutes, or until golden brown and firm to the touch. Remove them from the oven and let them cool for 5 minutes in the pan, then move them to a wire rack to cool completely.

4. Make the buttercream. Put the butter into a bowl and beat together with the confectioners' sugar until you have a creamy topping. Spread the frosting onto each cake.

5. Drizzle some melted chocolate onto the top of each one and top with a cherry half.

candy-top vanilla cupcakes

MAKES 18 CUPCAKES

FOR THE CUPCAKES
scant ⅔ cup butter, softened,
  or soft margarine
¾ cup superfine sugar
1½ tsp vanilla extract
2 large eggs, lightly beaten
¾ cup self-rising flour

FOR THE TOPPING
¾ cup soft butter
3 cups confectioners' sugar, sifted
a choice of your favorite small, soft
  candies, such as jelly beans

a crown of candies
fit for a princess

1. Turn on the oven to 375°F/190°C. Line two 12-hole muffin pans with 18 paper cupcake liners. Place the butter and sugar in a mixing bowl and beat together until light and fluffy, then beat in the vanilla extract. Gradually beat in the eggs, then sift in the flour and fold into the mixture. Spoon the mixture into the paper liners.

2. Bake in the preheated oven for 15-20 minutes, or until golden brown and firm to the touch. Remove them from the oven and let them cool for 5 minutes in the pan, then move them to a wire rack to cool completely.

3. Make the buttercream. Put the butter into a bowl and beat together with the confectioners' sugar until you have a creamy topping. Spread the frosting onto each cake. Arrange the candies on top to decorate.

vanilla frosted cupcakes

MAKES 12 CUPCAKES

FOR THE CUPCAKES
8 tbsp butter, softened
generous ½ cup superfine sugar
2 eggs, lightly beaten
generous ¾ cup self-rising flour
1 tbsp milk

FOR THE TOPPING
¾ cup unsalted butter, softened
1 tsp vanilla extract
2½ cups confectioners' sugar
1 tbsp colored sprinkles, to decorate

a sprinkling of sprinkles for extra sparkling cupcakes

1. Turn on the oven to 350°F/180°C. Put 12 paper cupcake liners in a muffin pan or put 12 double-layer paper liners on a baking sheet.

2. Put the butter and sugar into a mixing bowl and beat together until light and fluffy. Gradually beat in the eggs. Sift over the flour and, using a metal spoon, fold into the mixture with the milk. Spoon the mixture into the paper liners.

3. Bake in the preheated oven for 20 minutes, or until golden brown and firm to the touch. Remove them from the oven and let them cool for 5 minutes in the pan, then move them to a wire rack to cool completely.

4. To make the topping, put the butter and vanilla extract in a mixing bowl and beat until pale and soft. Gradually sift in the confectioners' sugar, beating well after each addition. Spoon the topping into a piping bag made with a large snip (see page 9). Squeeze swirls of the topping on the top of each cupcake, and finish with some sprinkles.

princess butterfly cakes

MAKES 12 CUPCAKES

FOR THE CUPCAKES
scant ½ cup soft butter
½ cup superfine sugar
2 eggs, lightly beaten
scant 1 cup self-rising flour, sifted
¼ cup unsweetened cocoa
  powder, sifted
½ tsp vanilla extract
1-2 tbsp milk

FOR THE TOPPING
¾ cup butter, softened
3 cups confectioners' sugar, sifted,
  plus a little extra for dusting
1-2 drops pink food coloring

butterflies that
will set even a
princess aflutter

1. Turn on the oven to 400°F/200°C. Put 12 paper cupcake liners in a 12-cup muffin pan.

2. Put the butter and superfine sugar into a mixing bowl and beat together for 1-2 minutes, until the mixture is pale and creamy. Gradually add the eggs and continue beating. Fold in the flour and unsweetened cocoa powder using a metal spoon. Stir in the vanilla extract and milk.

3. Put spoonfuls of the mixture into each paper liner. Bake in the preheated oven for 15-20 minutes, or until golden brown and firm to the touch. Remove them from the oven and let them cool for 5 minutes in the pan, then move them to a wire rack to cool completely.

4. Meanwhile, make the buttercream. Put the butter in a bowl and beat with the confectioners' sugar and food coloring until you have a smooth, creamy pink topping.

5. Cut a small circle from the top of each cake and cut it in half. Squeeze a swirl of the topping into the center of each cake, then place the 2 semicircles of cake on top like butterfly wings. Dust with a little confectioners' sugar.

fit for a princess!

magical recipes for cakes and
cookies to make a delicious,
twinkly princess snack.

blonde brownie hearts with raspberry sauce

MAKES 8 BROWNIES

FOR THE BROWNIES
oil, for oiling
1¼ cups all-purpose flour, plus extra
  for flouring
4 oz/115 g white chocolate,
  broken into pieces
8 tbsp unsalted butter
2 eggs, beaten
¾ cup superfine sugar
seeds from 1 vanilla bean
8 small squares
  bittersweet chocolate
whipped heavy cream, to serve
  (optional)

FOR THE RASPBERRY SAUCE
1½ cups raspberries,
  thawed if frozen
2 tbsp orange juice
1 tbsp confectioners' sugar

luscious chocolate
for the warmest
princess smile

1. Turn on the oven to 350°F/ 180°C. Oil and lightly flour 8 separate, heart-shaped baking pans, each holding ⅔ cup.

2. Place the chocolate and butter in a pan over low heat and heat gently, stirring, until just melted. Remove from the heat.

3. Beat together the eggs, sugar, and vanilla seeds until smooth and thick. Lightly fold in the flour, then stir in the chocolate mixture and mix evenly.

4. Pour the batter into the pans, adding a square of chocolate to the center of each, without pressing down. Bake in the preheated oven for 20-25 minutes, until just firm. Remove them from the oven and let them cool for 5 minutes. Run a knife around the edge of each heart to loosen it from the pan and turn them out onto individual plates.

5. Puree half the raspberries with the orange juice and confectioners` sugar, then push through a strainer to remove the seeds. Spoon the raspberry sauce around the cakes, decorate with the remaining raspberries, and serve warm, with whipped cream, if liked.

rocky road brownies

MAKES 16 BROWNIES

FOR THE BROWNIES
1 cup butter, melted, plus unmelted
  butter for greasing
scant 1 cup all-purpose flour, plus
  extra for dusting
scant ¾ cup superfine sugar
3 tbsp unsweetened cocoa powder
½ tsp baking powder
2 eggs, beaten
1 tsp vanilla extract
⅓ cup candied cherries,
  cut into fourths
⅔ cup blanched almonds, chopped
generous 1 cup chopped
  marshmallows, to decorate

FOR THE FUDGE TOPPING
1¾ cups confectioners' sugar
2 tbsp unsweetened cocoa
3 tbsp evaporated milk
½ tsp vanilla extract

cushioned with
marshmallows,
fit for a princess

1. Preheat the oven to 325°F/160°C. Grease a 9-inch/23-cm square, shallow cake pan and sprinkle lightly with flour.

2. Sift together the flour, sugar, cocoa, and baking powder and make a well in the center. Stir in the melted butter, eggs, and vanilla extract and beat well to mix thoroughly.

3. Stir in the cherries and almonds. Pour the mixture into the prepared pan and bake for 35-40 minutes, until just firm on top. Remove the brownies from the oven and let the brownies cool in the pan.

4. Meanwhile, make the topping. Place all the ingredients in a mixing bowl and beat well to mix to a smooth, just spreading consistency.

5. Spread the cooled brownies with the topping, swirling lightly, and sprinkle with marshmallows. Let stand until the topping sets, then cut into squares.

princess meringue kisses

MAKES ABOUT 30 MERINGUES

FOR THE MERINGUES
4 egg whites
generous 1 cup superfine sugar
1-2 drops pink food coloring
pink and silver sugar balls
  or pink sprinkles

TO SERVE
freshly whipped heavy cream
fresh strawberries

delicious kisses for
a delightful princess

1. Turn on the oven to 300°F/ 150°C. Line 2 baking trays with parchment paper (this will stop the meringues from sticking and means fewer things to wash).

2. Put the egg whites in a mixing bowl and use an electric handheld mixer to beat them until soft peaks form.

3. Gradually add the sugar, a spoonful at a time, beating well between each one, until all the sugar has been added. Add the food coloring until the mixture is evenly pink.

4. Put small spoonfuls of the meringue onto the baking trays and sprinkle a few sugar balls or sprinkles over each one.

5. Bake in the preheated oven for 1½ hours, until they are crisp and sound hollow when you tap the bottom of each one. Remove them from the oven and let them cool completely.

6. Serve the meringues piled up with a big bowl of whipped cream and some fresh strawberries.

sugared hearts

MAKES ABOUT 30 HEARTS

FOR THE COOKIES
1 cup butter, softened
scant ¾ cup superfine sugar
1 egg yolk, lightly beaten
2 tsp vanilla extract
2¼ cups all-purpose flour
¼ cup unsweetened cocoa powder
pinch of salt

FOR THE TOPPING
scant ¾ cup superfine sugar
pink food coloring paste
3½ oz/100 g semisweet chocolate,
  broken into pieces

sweet hearts
for a deserving
princess

1. Put the butter and sugar in a mixing bowl and mix, then beat in the egg yolk and vanilla extract. Sift the flour, cocoa powder, and salt into the mixture and stir until thoroughly combined. Halve the dough, shape into balls, and wrap in plastic wrap. Chill in the refrigerator for 30-60 minutes.

2. Turn on the oven to 375°F/190°C. Line 2 cookie sheets with parchment paper. Unwrap the dough and roll it out between 2 sheets of parchment paper. Cut out cookies using the heart template at the back of this book. Put them on the prepared cookie sheets, spaced apart. Bake for 10-15 minutes, until firm. Remove them from the oven and let cool on the cookie sheets for 10 minutes, then move to wire racks to cool completely.

3. For the topping, put the sugar in a plastic bag, add a little food coloring paste, seal, and rub together to mix. Then put the chocolate in a heatproof bowl and melt over a saucepan of simmering water (don't let the bowl touch the water). Remove from the heat and let cool slightly.

4. With the cookies still on the racks, spread the melted chocolate over them, then sprinkle with the colored sugar. Let set.

frosted stars

"superstars" for a
sparkling princess

MAKES ABOUT 30 STARS

FOR THE COOKIES
1 cup butter, softened
scant ¾ cup superfine sugar
1 egg yolk, lightly beaten
½ tsp vanilla extract
2½ cups all-purpose flour
pinch of salt

TO DECORATE
1¾ cups confectioners' sugar
1-2 tbsp water
a choice of candy-coated chocolate
   eggs, silver and gold balls, colored
   sprinkles, unsweetened dried coconut,
   sugar sprinkles, and sugar stars,
   hearts, and flowers

1. Put the butter and sugar into a bowl and mix well, then beat in the egg yolk and vanilla extract. Sift the flour and salt into the mixture and stir until combined. Halve the dough, shape into balls, and wrap in plastic wrap. Chill in the refrigerator for 30-60 minutes.

2. Turn on the oven to 375°F/ 190°C. Line 2 cookie sheets with parchment paper.

3. Unwrap the dough and roll it out between 2 sheets of parchment paper to 1/8 inch/3 mm thick. Stamp out cookies with a star-shaped cutter and put them on the cookie sheets spaced apart. Bake in the preheated oven for 10-15 minutes, until golden. Remove them from the oven and let them cool for 5-10 minutes in the pan, then move them to a wire rack to cool completely.

4. To decorate, sift the confectioners' sugar into a bowl and stir in the water until thick and creamy. Spread the frosting over the cookies, arrange your choice of decorations on top, and let set.

Push out the templates and use them to dust pretty patterns with confectioners' sugar on top of your cupcakes!

Princess party name plates

Push out the templates and place them on cardboard.

*

Draw around the outside of the template, then write the name
of your guest on each name plate. Decorate the name plates with
princess drawings, glitter, or sequins.

*

Ask Head Cook to help you cut out your name plates, then fold
along the dotted lines. Finally, add them to your princess party table!